LOBSTER
AND OTHER SHEL

ELAINE ELLIOT AND VIRGINIA LEE

Photographed on location by Steven Isleifson

FORMAC PUBLISHING COMPANY LIMITED
HALIFAX 1996

PHOTO CREDITS:
All photographs by Steven Isleifson except where noted below:
Keith Vaughan — pages 1, 3 (top only), 4–7, 31, 63.

PARTICIPATING RESTAURANTS:
Acton's Grill and Café, Wolfville, NS
Amherst Shore Country Inn, Lorneville, NS
Auberge Le Vieux Presbytère de Bouctouche 1880, Bouctouche, NB
Bellhill Tea House, Canning, NS
Blomidon Inn, Wolfville, NS
Bluenose Lodge, Lunenburg, NS
Compass Rose, Grand Manan, NB
Compass Rose Inn, Lunenburg, NS
Dalvay-by-the-Sea, Dalvay, PEI
Da Maurizio Dining Room, Halifax, NS
Drury Lane Steakhouse, Aulac, NB
Dufferin Inn and San Martello Diningroom, Saint John, NB
Duncreigan Country Inn, Mabou, NS
Dunes Café and Gardens, Brackley Beach, PEI
Haddon Hall, Chester, NS
Halliburton House Inn, Halifax, NS
Inn at Bay Fortune, Bay Fortune, PEI
Inn on the Cove, Saint John, NB
Inn on the Lake, Waverley, NS
La Perla Restaurant, Dartmouth, NS
Marshlands Inn, Sackville, NB
Mountain Gap Inn and Resort, Smith's Cove, NS
Murray Manor Bed and Breakfast, Yarmouth, NS
Nemo's Restaurant, Halifax, NS
Off-Broadway Café, Charlottetown, PEI
Quaco Inn, St. Martins, NB
Scanway Restaurant, Halifax, NS
Shaw's Hotel, Brackley Beach, PEI

Dedication:

This book is dedicated to the memory of our parents, Margaret and Frank Stuart, who instilled in us a love of the Maritime way of life and taught us to believe in ourselves.

Formac Publishing Company Limited acknowledges the support of the Department of Canadian Heritage and the Nova Scotia Department of Education and Culture in the development of writing and publishing in Canada.

Canadian Cataloguing in Publication Data
Elliot, Elaine, 1939-
      Lobster and other shellfish
      (Maritime flavours series)
      ISBN 0-88780-354-7
1. Cookery (Lobsters). 2. Cookery (Shellfish). 3. Cookery, Canadian -- Maritime Provinces.
I. Lee, Virginia, 1947- . II. Title. III. Series.
TX753.B5E44 1996   641.6'92   C95-950018-1

Formac Publishing Company Limited
5502 Atlantic Street
Halifax, N.S.
B3H 1G4

Distributed in the United States by:
Seven Hills Book Distributors
49 Central Avenue
Cincinnati, OH   45202

CONTENTS

INTRODUCTION *4*

APPETIZERS *9*

PASTA AND LIGHTER FARE *19*

THE MAIN COURSE 41

INDEX *64*

INTRODUCTION

The very warm reception accorded our 1994 book, *Maritime Flavours Guidebook and Cookbook*, demonstrated that interest in the cuisine of the Maritime region is flourishing. The book also showed how you can prepare at home the innovative recipes that professional chefs have developed in all three provinces.

In our visits to inns and restaurants over the years, one thing that has impressed us is the wide range of ideas that our best chefs have for including regional specialities. For this reason we decided to develop a series of four books that would celebrate the wonderful bounty of land and sea, in particular apples, blueberries, salmon, and lobster and other shellfish. We visited many of the inns and restaurants featured in *Maritime Flavours* and once again, the chefs gave us a generous selection of recipes with which to work. We selected the ones that would give you a wide range of choice for enjoying the flavours of the region. To round out each book, we added some tried and true recipes from our personal collections. All recipes in this book have been tested in our homes and the quantities adjusted to serve four to six adults. For some recipes we have suggested low-fat alternatives.

Fine food presentation is an art, and one which is receiving increased emphasis by our chefs. What better way to describe how these recipes are presented by their originators than to show you! Photographer Steven Isleifson visited our featured restaurants and photographed the dishes found in this *Maritime Flavours* series. What you see in these pages are the dishes as they are presented by their chefs, photographed on location.

Lobster is, of course, king of the Maritime crustaceans. Our all-time favourite way to enjoy lobster is to buy it live and cook it at the beach. Alas, Nova Scotia's climate renders this adventure rather unlikely during most of the year, hence we prepare it in our kitchens or sample the offerings of the chefs of our restaurants and inns.

In addition to the lobster dishes, we have included a few recipes featuring crab, scallops, shrimp, clams and the cultivated blue mussel. Whether you choose a chowder, dip, pasta dish or elaborate main entrée, we are sure this book will include offerings for every palate. Enjoy!

BUYING AND STORING

LOBSTER — available live, fresh cooked, frozen, canned

When purchasing live lobster ensure that the feelers and claws move and the tail springs back when straightened. The colour may range from blue to mottled green.

Cooked lobster should have a bright red shell and fresh aroma. Store live lobster in refrigerator for 12 to 24 hours. Cover with a damp cloth. Do not immerse in water or set on ice.

Cooked lobster keeps for up to two days in the refrigerator, but we recommend using it as soon as possible. Freeze lobster meat in a brine solution of 2 teaspoons of salt to 1 cup water, in tightly sealed containers with 1/2-inch headspace for expansion. Do not keep longer than 2 months in the freezer. Lobster left in its shell can be frozen in an airtight freezer bag. Thaw unopened containers in refrigerator, or in cold water bath. Never thaw at room temperature nor refreeze.

CRAB — available live, fresh cooked, frozen, canned

Crab has a short survival time out of ocean water. If purchasing live crab, look for claw movement and cook immediately. It is most often sold fresh-cooked, canned or frozen.

Store live crab in refrigerator covered with wet newspaper or damp cloth for up to 12 hours.

Cooked crab meat keeps refrigerated for 24 hours. Freeze crab meat in a brine solution of 2 teaspoons salt to 1 cup water, in tightly sealed containers with 1/2-inch headspace for expansion. Do not keep longer than 2 months in the freezer. Thaw unopened containers in refrigerator or in cold water bath. Never thaw at room temperature or refreeze.

SCALLOPS — available fresh, frozen

Scallops are caught and immediately shucked (shelled). Look for large, white or pink fleshed meat that is moist and not odorous.

Store fresh scallops in tightly covered container in refrigerator for 1 to 2 days. To freeze scallops, wash in brine (1 tablespoon salt to 4 cups water), drain and package in freezer bags. Store up to 3 months in the freezer. Thaw unopened bags in refrigerator or in cold water bath just until scallops can be separated. Never thaw at room temperature or refreeze.

MUSSELS AND CLAMS — live in shell, shucked, canned

Live mussels and clams should have a closed shell. Those exposed to air will gape slightly but should close when sharply tapped. Molluscs that do not close are dead and must be discarded.

Store live, covered with a damp cloth, for up to 24 hours in refrigerator. Do not store in sealed plastic bags. Refrigerate shucked mussels or clams with their liquor in tightly covered containers for no longer than 2 days. Freeze shucked meat up to 4 months. Thaw in refrigerator overnight.

SHRIMP — available fresh, frozen

Canadian shrimp are generally small. The medium to large shrimp sold commercially are imported. Raw shrimp are grey, green or pink in colour and turn pink when cooked. "Deveined" shrimp have the sand vein, running down the dorsal side, removed.

Store cooked or uncooked shrimp in a refrigerator no longer than 3 days. To freeze shrimp: shell, remove sand vein, wash in brine (1 tablespoon salt to 4 cups water), drain and package in plastic freezer bags. Store up to 3 months in the freezer. Thaw unopened bags in refrigerator or in cold water bath just until shrimp can be separated. Never thaw at room temperature or refreeze.

LOBSTER

We draw the line when it comes to cooking lobster by any other means than boiling or steaming. In our extensive research we have learned that, indeed, lobster may be cooked in the microwave oven, cut open live and broiled, severed at the spine, and so on. We offer the traditional Maritime method for preparing fresh-caught lobster.

Fill a large pot with enough salted water to cover lobsters and bring to a full boil. Grab lobster by the back and plunge, head first into the boiling water. Cover pot. When water returns to a boil, reduce heat to medium and cook 12 minutes for the first pound and 4 minutes for each additional pound of lobster. When fully cooked, antennae can easily be pulled out. Remove from pot, cool shell under running cold water and serve.

(Directions for cooking other shellfish featured in this book are found in individual recipes.)

NUTRITIONAL VALUES

Shellfish are high in protein, have negligible amounts of saturated fat and are low in cholesterol and calories. They contain valuable amounts of iron, zinc, calcium, magnesium and iodine, as well as Vitamin A. In addition, shellfish contain Omega 3 polyunsaturated fatty acids which significantly reduce blood clotting, lowering the risk of heart attack and stroke. A 3.5 ounce serving of boiled or steamed shellfish contains between 74 and 93 calories.

Lobster
3.5 oz. serving cooked with moist heat (steamed or boiled)

Calories	91 kcal
Polyunsaturated fat	0.09 g
Cholesterol	95 mg
Omega 3	.38 g

Atlantic Snow or Queen Crab
3.5 oz. serving cooked with moist heat (steamed or boiled)

Calories	90 kcal
Polyunsaturated fat	0.42 g
Cholesterol	76 mg
Omega 3	.30 g

Scallops
3.5 oz. serving cooked with moist heat

Calories	88 kcal
Polyunsaturated fat	0.24 g
Cholesterol	33 mg
Omega 3	.44 g

Shrimp
3.5 oz. serving cooked with moist heat

Calories	92 kcal
Polyunsaturated fat	0.70 g
Cholesterol	153 mg
Omega 3	.50 g

Mussels
3.5 oz. serving cooked with moist heat

Calories	86 kcal
Polyunsaturated fat	0.61 g
Cholesterol	28 mg
Omega 3	.36 g

Clams
3.5 oz. serving cooked with moist heat

Calories	74 kcal
Polyunsaturated fat	0.44 g
Cholesterol	65.6 mg
Omega 3	.38 g

APPETIZERS
& SOUPS

*I*n our travels throughout the region we have found talented chefs utilizing the ocean's bounty in a variety of first course dishes. From soups and chowders to salads and elegant appetizers, we are sure that you will want to try their creations.

◀ *Chef Scott Carr's Seafood Chowder with Lobster as served at the Dunes Café and Gardens.*

DUNES' SEAFOOD CHOWDER WITH LOBSTER

THE DUNES CAFÉ AND GARDENS, BRACKLEY BEACH, PEI

Scott Carr, Chef at the Dunes, prepares his fish stock in advance. While we offer his directions for stock, novice cooks can substitute bottled clam juice or stock made from powdered fish bouillon. You can reduce the fat content in this chowder by substituting light cream or milk in place of heavy cream.

4 cups fish stock (recipe follows)

4 tablespoons butter

4 tablespoons flour

1/8 teaspoon nutmeg

salt and white pepper, to taste

4 large potatoes, peeled, and cut in large dice

4 tablespoons butter (2nd amount)

1/2 cup onion, chopped

1/2 cup celery, chopped

1 can frozen lobster meat (11.3 ounces)

3 ounces salmon fillet, in small chunks

3 ounces sole or haddock fillets, in small chunks

4 ounces shrimp, shelled

1/2 pound mussels, steamed and shelled

1 cup heavy cream (35% mf)

Place fish stock in a large pot and heat to a simmer. Combine butter and flour to make a paste. Whisk butter mixture into hot stock, bring to a boil and cook 2 minutes, stirring constantly. Season with nutmeg, salt and pepper; set aside.

Cook potato cubes gently in salted water until just tender. Drain and reserve.

Melt second amount of butter in a skillet and sauté onion and celery until soft. Stir in juice from frozen lobster, and all of the seafood. Simmer 3 minutes. Combine seafood and reserved potatoes with thickened fish stock, adjust seasonings if necessary. Add cream and bring to serving temperature. Do not boil. Serves 4–6.

Fish Stock

6 cups water

1 pound fish bones

1 bay leaf

3 whole cloves

1 medium onion, peeled

Place water and fish bones in a large kettle. Stick bay leaf and cloves into onion and add to pot. Bring to a boil, reduce heat and simmer 20 minutes. Strain.

HOT ATLANTIC CRAB DIP

Easily prepared in advance, this dish has become a favourite at social gatherings. We are sure this dip will disappear quickly from your buffet table when your friends arrive!

1 can frozen Atlantic crab (11 ounces), thawed and drained

8 ounces cream cheese, softened

4 tablespoons egg-based mayonnaise

salt and pepper, to taste

assorted crackers

Pick over crab to remove any shell or cartilage. Blend crab, cream cheese and mayonnaise; season with salt and pepper. Turn into a shallow baking dish, cover and refrigerate. At serving time preheat oven to 325°F and bake 30 minutes or until browned on top and bubbly. Serve with assorted crackers. Yields 2 cups.

LEMON STEAMED MUSSELS

Jack Sorenson, now of the Innlet Café, perfected this recipe several years ago when he and his wife Katherine operated The Zwicker Inn in Mahone Bay.

3 pounds cultivated mussels

6 tablespoons unsalted butter

2 tablespoons flour

4 tablespoons grated carrot

2 tablespoons chopped green onion

2 tablespoons chopped parsley

1 garlic clove, minced

1/4 teaspoon pepper

1/4 cup water

1 lemon thinly sliced

Scrub and debeard mussels in cold running water, discarding any that are open or have broken shells. Combine all ingredients except mussels in a large saucepan and bring to a boil, stirring constantly. Add mussels and stir to coat them evenly with sauce. Cover and steam for 5–7 minutes, being careful not to overcook. Remove mussels to two large bowls, discarding any that have not opened. Top with sauce. Serves 2.

GAZPACHO WITH LOBSTER

HADDON HALL, CHESTER, NS

The Chef at Haddon Hall likes to add a Mediterranean touch to his summer menu during the hot sunny days of August! Remember, the soup is prepared and chilled for about 12 hours to allow the flavours to blend.

1 onion

1 garlic clove

1/2 English-style cucumber, pared and seeded

1 green pepper, in chunks

4 – 5 large vine-ripened tomatoes, blanched, peeled and seeded

1/2 cup oil

1/4 cup vinegar

2 cups water

1 1/2 teaspoons sweet paprika

1 slice of bread

pinch of caraway seeds

4 whole pepper corns

salt, to taste

4 ounces fresh lobster meat, in bite-size pieces

Combine all ingredients except lobster and process in batches in a food processor or blender. Refrigerate 10–12 hours. Serve in chilled soup bowls topped with fresh lobster chunks. Serves 4.

Chillled Gazpacho with lobster as served at Haddon Hall, Chester, NS. ▶

LOBSTER STUFFED MUSHROOM CAPS

THE OFF BROADWAY CAFÉ, CHARLOTTETOWN, PEI

Peter Williams of the Off Broadway Café serves mushroom caps stuffed with lobster, drizzled with a rich Béarnaise Sauce and topped with grated Jarlsberg cheese. We suggest making this decadent appetizer for a special occasion.

16 large mushroom caps, stems removed

2 tablespoons butter

2 tablespoons butter (2nd amount)

2 tablespoons flour

1/2 cup heavy cream (35% mf)

1 tablespoon dry white vermouth

2 tablespoons lobster or fish broth

scant pinch nutmeg

pinch cayenne pepper

1 teaspoon paprika

8 ounces fresh lobster meat, in small pieces

Béarnaise Sauce, recipe follows

1/2 cup grated Jarlsberg cheese

Clean mushroom caps. Melt 2 tablespoons butter in a skillet over medium heat and sauté mushrooms until slightly browned and tender. Place mushrooms in a single layer in the bottom of a shallow baking dish. Set aside.

Melt second amount of butter in a large saucepan. Whisk in flour and cook until roux is bubbly and slightly browned, about 5 minutes. Stir in cream, vermouth and broth; cook, stirring constantly until thickened. Season with nutmeg, pepper and paprika. Fold in lobster meat and spoon into mushroom caps. Top each mushroom with a tablespoon of Béarnaise Sauce, sprinkle with grated cheese and broil, 6 inches from the element until hot and bubbly. Serves 4–6.

Béarnaise Sauce

3 egg yolks

1 teaspoon lemon juice

1 1/2 teaspoon cider vinegar

1/2 teaspoon dried tarragon

1/2 cup unsalted butter, melted

In a food processor, blend egg yolks, lemon juice, vinegar and tarragon for 10 seconds. Continue to process and slowly add melted butter in a steady stream. Serve immediately.

ATLANTIC MUSSELS IN CREAMY HERB SAUCE

This steamed mussel recipe is bound to become a favourite. We suggest you have lots of warm, crusty bread on the table to dip in the delicious sauce.

Sauce

1 tablespoon butter

1 tomato, seeded and coarsely chopped

1 garlic clove, minced

2 green onions, chopped

salt and pepper, to taste

2 tablespoons fresh basil, chopped or
1 1/2 teaspoons dried

1 cup heavy cream

Melt butter in a small saucepan and sauté tomato and garlic for 2–3 minutes. Add green onions, seasonings and cream. Bring to a boil and reduce by one half, about 4 minutes. Set aside.

2–3 pounds fresh Atlantic mussels, scrubbed and debearded

2 tablespoons butter

1/2 small onion, finely chopped

1 garlic clove, minced

1 bay leaf

1 teaspoon pepper

1/2 cup dry white wine

Prepare mussels, discarding any with broken shells. Melt butter in a large stockpot and sauté onion and garlic over medium heat for 2 minutes. Add bay leaf, pepper and wine. Bring to a simmer, add mussels. Cover and steam 5–7 minutes or until mussel shells open. Strain broth into a separate pot, bring to a boil and reduce by one third, about 3 minutes. Add reserved cream sauce and boil 2 minutes. To serve, discard any mussels that have not opened. Remove the upper part of each shell. Place mussel in shells in bowls and drizzle with cream sauce. Serves 4.

Cozze al Forno (Broiled Mussels)

LA PERLA RESTAURANT, DARTMOUTH, NS

At La Perla, these mussels are drizzled with additional garlic butter. For an elegant presentation, serve them nestled on a platter of rock salt.

12 ounces fresh spinach, washed and stemmed

2 pounds fresh mussels, scrubbed and debearded

2 tablespoons garlic butter

1/2 cup onion, finely chopped

1/2 cup ricotta cheese

salt and pepper, to taste

3 ounces provolone cheese, grated

Blanch spinach for 30 seconds. Cool, squeeze out excess moisture and chop. Reserve.

Steam prepared mussels in 1/4 cup water until shells open, about 5 minutes. Discard any that do not open. Refresh in cold water and remove half the shell so you are left with a mussel on the half-shell.

Preheat oven broiler. In a medium-sized skillet, melt garlic butter and sauté onion until translucent. Add spinach and cook 2 minutes. Stir in ricotta, salt and pepper. Remove from heat, cool, and add provolone. Arrange mussels on a large baking tray. Top mussels with spinach mixture and place under broiler until hot. Drizzle with additional melted garlic butter, if desired. Serves 4.

Creamy Clam Chowder

SHAW'S HOTEL, BRACKLEY BEACH, PEI

To lessen the fat content, we also tested this recipe substituting light for heavy cream. While the soup was not as rich, it retained its wonderful flavour.

1/2 cup celery, chopped

1/2 cup onion, chopped

1/2 cup butter

3 tablespoons flour

2 cups milk

1/2 cup heavy cream (35% mf) or light cream (10% mf)

2 tablespoons powdered chicken stock base

1 pound clam meat and liquor (2 cans clams with juice)

1 cup pre-cooked potatoes, diced

2 tablespoons pimento, chopped

2 tablespoons fresh parsley, chopped

In a large saucepan, sauté the celery and onion in butter until tender, being careful not to allow the vegetables to brown. Whisk in the flour to form a roux and incorporate milk, cream and chicken stock, stirring constantly. Add clams and liquor, potatoes, pimento and parsley and cook over medium heat until hot and slightly thickened. Do not boil. Serves 6–8.

ATLANTIC BLUE MUSSEL CHOWDER

What a wonderful way to utilize the famous Maritime mussels. The subtle flavour of this golden chowder is enhanced by the addition of curry.

2 pounds fresh mussels

1/2 cup dry white wine

1/4 cup shallots, finely chopped

1/3 cup onion, finely chopped

a few sprigs of parsley and dill

1/4 bay leaf

2 tablespoons butter

1/2 cup celery, julienne

1/2 cup carrot, julienne

2 cups fish stock

3/4 cup heavy cream (35% mf)

1 egg yolk, beaten

1 tablespoon curry powder or to taste

salt and freshly ground pepper, to taste

Scrub and debeard the mussels, being careful to discard any that are open or have broken shells. In a large pot bring to a boil wine, shallots, onion, parsley, dill and bay leaf. Add mussels and steam, covered, for 5 minutes or until they open. Strain cooking liquid through cheesecloth and reserve. Discard any mussels that do not fully open. Remove mussels from shells and reserve.

In a separate heavy-bottomed saucepan, melt butter and sauté celery and carrots until softened. Remove with a slotted spoon and reserve. Add fish stock and mussel liquid to saucepan; bring to a boil and reduce by half. Add cream, mussels and julienne vegetables and remove from heat. Stir a small amount of hot mixture into beaten egg yolk, return to hot mixture. Add curry powder, season with salt and pepper and return to serving temperature, being careful not to boil. Serves 4.

PASTA &
LIGHTER FARE

*I*f you have a busy lifestyle you might want to try one of these luncheon and "one-dish" meals. Crab Crèpes with Lemon Caper Sauce and Pasta Alberoni from Bellhill Tea House, served with a salad, are excellent choices for a light dinner.

◀ Lobster Linguini from the Blomidon Inn, Wolfville, NS — a tasty luncheon dish.

LOBSTER LINGUINI

BLOMIDON INN, WOLFVILLE, NS

We questioned the chef at the Blomidon Inn on the quantity of horseradish in this recipe and were assured that, indeed, it was the proper amount. This delicious, easily-prepared lobster entrée has an unforgettable flavour.

1 tablespoon butter

12 ounces fresh or 1 can frozen lobster meat

2/3 cup chopped tomatoes

4 tablespoons creamed horseradish

1/4 cup dry white wine

3 cups heavy cream (35% mf)

1/4 cup chopped green onions

salt & pepper to taste

1 pound fresh linguini pasta

In a heavy skillet, over medium high heat, heat butter and sauté lobster, tomatoes and horseradish until tomatoes are softened. Remove lobster and tomatoes with a slotted spoon and reserve.

Deglaze skillet with wine. Add cream, bring to a boil and reduce to a slightly thickened sauce consistency. Add green onions, reserved lobster and tomatoes and season with salt and pepper.

In a large pot of boiling salted water, cook pasta until al dente (tender yet firm). Drain pasta and serve on warmed plates topped with lobster cream sauce. Serves 4–6.

SEAFOOD LASAGNA

THE COMPASS ROSE, GRAND MANAN, NB

Guests at Grand Manan's The Compass Rose are treated to spectacular seafood, fresh from the docks at North Head. We tested this recipe using light cottage cheese and milk in place of the cream. While the dish was not as rich, we were delighted with the results.

10 lasagna noodles

1 1/2 pounds mixed seafood (e.g., lobster, scallops, shrimp, crab, salmon, white fish)

1 pound fresh spinach

4 eggs

1 pound cottage cheese

salt and pepper to taste

1/8 teaspoon nutmeg

6 tablespoons butter

1 onion, chopped

1 clove garlic, crushed

1 tablespoon fresh dill

6 tablespoons flour

salt and pepper to taste

2 tablespoons sherry

3 cups light cream (10% mf)

1 cup grated Swiss cheese

1/2 cup grated Parmesan cheese

Cook lasagna noodles until tender, drain and rinse under cold water, set aside. In boiling salted water, poach raw seafood until barely cooked. Drain and reserve. Briefly blanch spinach, drain well and chop. Lightly beat eggs. In a large bowl combine eggs, spinach and cottage cheese. Season with salt, pepper and nutmeg. Set aside.

Preheat oven to 350°F. Melt butter and sauté onion and garlic until soft. Add dill, flour, salt and pepper and cook, stirring constantly over medium heat for one minute. Whisk sherry and cream into flour mixture, a little at a time, until smooth and well blended. Cook, stirring constantly, until thickened. Add Swiss cheese and seafood to sauce, stirring until cheese is melted.

To assemble place half the noodles in a greased 9 x 13-inch lasagna pan. Spread half the spinach mixture over noodles and cover with half the seafood sauce. Repeat layers and top with grated Parmesan cheese. Bake 45 minutes to an hour, or until bubbly and lightly browned. Remove from oven and let stand 10–15 minutes before serving. Serves 6–8.

DRURY LANE CLUB SANDWICH

DRURY LANE STEAKHOUSE,
AULAC, NB

These club sandwiches are a hit with customers at Drury Lane. The staff like to promote them at lunchtime, commenting, "They make for good tips!"

three slices of white bread, toasted

shredded lettuce

thin tomato slices

3 strips of bacon, cooked crisp and drained

4 ounces lobster meat

mayonnaise

Spread first slice of toast with mayonnaise and cover with lettuce, tomato, and bacon. Cover with second slice of toast, spread mayonnaise and lobster meat. Spread mayonnaise on one side of the third slice of toast and top sandwich. To serve, cut in quarters and secure with a toothpick. Garnish as desired. Serves 1.

A Club House Sandwich with style, served at Drury Lane Steakhouse, Aulac, NB. ▶

LOBSTER ROLL

MOUNTAIN GAP INN AND RESORT, SMITH'S COVE, NS

This traditional Maritime Lobster Roll is served with fries and coleslaw. We tested the sandwich using Cecilia Bowden's roll recipe from The Compass Rose, Grand Manan Island.

3 cups cooked lobster meat, in bite-sized pieces

1/4 cup celery, chopped fine

mayonnaise

salt and pepper to taste

shredded lettuce

4 "lobster" rolls (recipe follows)

Fold together lobster and celery with just enough mayonnaise to bind them. Season with salt and pepper. Split four rolls almost through and toast lightly. Place lettuce on rolls and fill with lobster mixture. Serves 4.

"Lobster" Rolls

THE COMPASS ROSE, GRAND MANAN, NB

1 tablespoon dry yeast

1 teaspoon sugar

1/2 cup lukewarm water

1/3 cup sugar

1 teaspoon salt

1/3 cup oil

1 2/3 cups warm water

5 – 6 cups white flour

1 tablespoon butter

Dissolve yeast and 1 teaspoon sugar in lukewarm water and let rise to at least 1 cup in volume. Combine sugar, salt, oil and warm water in a large bowl and whisk briskly. Add yeast mixture to other liquids and beat. Gradually add flour, 1 cup at a time, beating after each addition, until you need to combine the remainder with your hands.

Turn out on a flour covered surface and knead until smooth and slightly sticky, about 5 minutes. Place dough in a greased bowl and turn to cover with oil. Cover and let rise for 45 minutes in a warm, draft-free place.

Punch down and shape into 12 oblong rolls. Place on a greased cookie sheet, cover loosely and let rise again for 45 minutes.

Preheat oven to 375°F. Bake rolls 12–15 minutes until slightly golden. Remove from oven, brush tops with butter and cool on wire racks. Yields 12 "lobster" rolls.

Traditional Maritime Lobster Roll served in the dining room of Mountain Gap Inn, ▶
Smiths Cove, NS.

LOBSTER ON POTATO PANCAKES WITH SOUR CREAM SAUCE

DUFFERIN INN AND SAN MARTELLO DININGROOM, SAINT JOHN, NB

Owners Margret and Axel Begner give a European flavour to Atlantic lobster with these potato pancakes accompanied by sour cream sauce.

3 medium-sized potatoes, peeled

1 tablespoon flour

1 egg, slightly beaten

pinch of salt

vegetable oil for frying

1 1/2 cups fresh lobster meat

Grate potatoes into a large bowl. Stir in flour and beaten egg. Heat a skillet and brush with a small amount of oil. Drop heaping tablespoon of potato mixture onto hot skillet and fry pancake until golden brown on one side. Flip pancake, press with a spatula to flatten, and fry until golden. Remove from skillet, set on paper towels to remove any excess oil and keep warm.

To serve, arrange pancakes on individual plates, top with lobster and nap with sour cream sauce. Serves 4 – 6.

Sour Cream Sauce

1/2 cup sour cream

1/2 teaspoon prepared horseradish

1/2 teaspoon lemon juice

pinch of sugar

1 green onion, thinly sliced

salt and pepper to taste

Combine all ingredients in a small bowl and whisk until blended. Refrigerate.

Lobster on Potato Pancakes with a Sour Cream Sauce from the San Martello Dining Room ▶
of the Dufferin Inn, Saint John, NB.

NOVE SCOTIA-STYLE CREAMED LOBSTER

THE MURRAY MANOR BED AND
BREAKFAST, YARMOUTH, NS

*In Yarmouth, where lobster is plentiful, every cook
has her own special recipe. Joan Semple serves her
rendition on toast points or over rice, accompanied
by a fresh green salad.*

3–4 cups lobster meat, preferably fresh

3 tablespoons butter

1 cup heavy cream (35% mf)

1/2 teaspoon paprika

6–8 sprigs fresh parsley, chopped

salt and pepper, to taste

Pick over lobster pieces being sure to remove
any cartilage or shell. Cut into bite-size pieces.

Melt butter in a skillet over medium heat. Add
cream and paprika, and take care not to boil.
Add lobster and parsley; season with salt and
pepper. Return to serving temperature. Spoon
over cooked rice or toast points. Serves 4–6.

LOBSTER TOAST POINTS

INN ON THE LAKE, WAVERLEY, NS

*This dish is served at the inn with fresh parsley
and a side salad. It provides an ample luncheon
serving or light dinner entrée.*

1/4 pound fresh mushrooms, diced

8–12 ounces cooked lobster meat, in bite-size
chunks

3 tablespoons grated carrot

2 1/2 tablespoons fish stock

1/2 teaspoon sweet Hungarian paprika (or to
taste)

1 cup heavy cream (35% mf)

1/4 pound cheddar cheese, grated

4 thick slices white bread, toasted

8 fresh parsley sprigs, chopped

Combine mushrooms, lobster, carrot, stock,
paprika and cream in a large saucepan and
cook over medium heat until slightly
thickened. Add cheese and stir until melted.
Toast bread, cut in wedges and serve lobster
mixture spooned over toast, garnished with
fresh parsley. Serves 4.

Lobster served on Toast Points with a mixed salad at Inn on the Lake, Waverley, NS. ▶

CRAB CRÈPES WITH LEMON CAPER SAUCE

This impressive luncheon dish is both inexpensive and easy to prepare. We found that the Lemon Caper Sauce is equally delicious served with other seafood.

2 tablespoons butter

1 tablespoon vegetable oil

1 small onion, diced

1 small green pepper, diced

1 clove garlic, crushed

4 ounces cooked ham, finely chopped

8 ounces crab meat

1 tablespoon brandy (optional)

salt and freshly ground pepper to taste

Preheat over to 350°F. Heat butter and oil in a skillet, add onion, green pepper and garlic and sauté until vegetables are softened but not browned. Add ham and crab meat and cook for 1 minute; stir in brandy. Remove from heat, add salt and pepper to taste and reserve.

Basic Crèpe Recipe

The crèpes may be made in advance; separate with waxed paper, wrap tightly in foil and freeze. To thaw, simply remove quantity needed and bring to room temperature.

2 eggs

1 cup milk

3/4 cup flour

pinch of salt

Whisk together eggs and milk. Add flour and salt and continue beating until the batter is smooth. Rest batter for 1 hour.

Brush a non-stick skillet with a little vegetable oil and bring to a medium heat. Add enough batter to barely cover the bottom of the pan (scant 1/4 cup) and cook for approximately 30 seconds. Flip crèpe and cook another 15 seconds. Repeat, setting crèpes aside to cool. Makes approximately 1 dozen large or 16 medium crèpes.

Lemon Caper Sauce

1 cup chicken broth

1/3 cup butter

3 tablespoons fresh lemon juice

1 egg yolk, beaten

1 tablespoon water

2 teaspoons cornstarch

3 teaspoons capers, drained and chopped

white pepper to taste

Bring broth, butter and lemon juice to a boil over medium high heat, stirring until the butter melts. Reduce heat to low. Blend egg, water and cornstarch until creamy. Stir small amount of hot mixture into egg, return to hot mixture and cook, stirring constantly until thickened. Do not boil. Remove from heat, stir in capers and season to taste with pepper. Serve warm.

To assemble, divide crab filling between crèpes and roll up, enclosing the ends. Place seam side down in a greased shallow baking dish, cover with foil and bake 15 minutes. Serve with warm Lemon Caper Sauce. Serves 4.

LOBSTER AND SCALLOPS WITH SUN-DRIED TOMATOES IN BASIL CREAM

DUNCREIGAN COUNTRY INN, MABOU, NS

Sun-dried tomatoes are available in speciality stores, either dry or oil-packed. If using the dry variety, reconstitute in a little warm water to soften, then drain. Always drain tomatoes that are packed in oil.

3/4 pound large scallops

4 tablespoons butter

3 to 4 shallots, minced

4 cooked lobster tails, split

1/2 cup white wine

1/2 cup sun-dried tomatoes, reconstituted (or well-drained, seeded, chopped tomatoes)

4 tablespoons fresh basil, chopped

salt and pepper, to taste

dash of cayenne

1/2 cup heavy cream (35% mf)

4 ounces Havarti cheese, grated

fresh pasta to serve 4

Sauté scallops in butter over medium high heat for 1 minute. Add shallots and split lobster tails. Bring to a simmer and cook only until scallops are done, about 2 additional minutes. Remove from pan and keep warm. Deglaze pan with wine, add tomatoes and basil. Season with salt, pepper and cayenne. Add cream and reduce sauce to slightly thicken. Stir in cheese and heat to melt. Return seafood to sauce and serve immediately over prepared pasta. Serves 4.

Chef Eleanor Mullendore's Lobster and Scallops with Sun-dried Tomatoes in Basil Cream, ▼
at the Duncreigan Country Inn, Mabou, NS.

FRESH ATLANTIC LOBSTER SOUFFLÉ

ACTON'S GRILL AND CAFÉ, WOLFVILLE, NS

At Acton's this soufflé is accompanied by assorted greens dressed with a fresh herb vinaigrette. Always serve a soufflé straight from the oven, before it collapses.

16 cups water

1 tablespoon salt

1 medium onion, peeled and halved

1 medium carrot, peeled and diced

2 stalks celery

2 small bay leaves

4 whole cloves

6 whole allspice

2–3 tomatoes, cut in chunks

1 tablespoon paprika

1 1/2 pound lobster

2 tablespoons unsalted butter

2 tablespoons flour

1 cup reserved lobster stock, warm

1/4 cup heavy cream (35% mf), warmed

1/4 teaspoon lemon juice

1 tablespoon brandy

6 whole eggs, separated

salt and freshly ground white pepper, to taste

Pour water into large stockpot. Add salt, onion, carrot, celery, bay, cloves, allspice, tomatoes, paprika and bring to a boil; reduce heat and simmer 15 minutes. Return to full boil, add lobster, cover and cook 15 minutes. Remove lobster from pot and set aside to cool. Keep stock hot.

Twist the tail and claws from the lobster body. Remove meat from shells, cut into small chunks and reserve. Split body in half, place in stockpot and return to a boil. Reduce heat and simmer 1 hour. Strain, discarding solids and reserving stock.

Preheat oven to 400°F. In a heavy saucepan melt butter and whisk in flour. Cook over low heat for one minute, add 1 cup reserved lobster stock and cream. Bring to a boil, whisking constantly until sauce thickens. Remove from heat, whisk in lemon juice, brandy and egg yolks. Add lobster meat, salt and pepper and set aside.

Butter and lightly flour a 2-quart soufflé dish. Beat egg whites until stiff but not dry, then gently fold into the lobster mixture. Pour into dish and bake 15–20 minutes until puffed and browned. Serve immediately. Yields 4 servings.

A picture perfect Fresh Atlantic Lobster Soufflé from Acton's Grill and Café, Wolfville, NS. ▶

PASTA ALBERONI

BELLHILL TEA HOUSE, CANNING, NS

This tasty Italian-style lobster casserole makes a great luncheon or supper dish when served with a green vegetable and warm Italian bread.

1/4 pound fresh mushrooms, sliced

2 tablespoons butter

3/4 pound lobster meat in bite-sized pieces (drain well if frozen)

1/2 cup white wine

salt and pepper to taste

2 tablespoons butter (2nd amount)

2 tablespoons flour

dash of grated nutmeg

1 cup milk

2/3 cup Parmesan cheese

1/4 pound mozzarella cheese, grated

3/4 pound penne pasta

butter (3rd amount)

freshly grated pepper

Preheat oven to 375°F. In a small skillet sauté mushrooms in 2 tablespoons butter, until softened. Add lobster and wine, and season with salt and pepper. Remove from heat and reserve.

In another saucepan, over medium heat, melt 2 tablespoons butter (2nd amount) and whisk in flour and nutmeg, combining well. Slowly add milk, stirring constantly to prevent lumps. Continue to cook until sauce thickens and begins to boil. Fold lobster mixture and half the Parmesan cheese into sauce. Remove from heat.

Prepare pasta according to package directions until almost cooked. Drain pasta thoroughly and add to sauce. Butter a 2-quart casserole and add one third of the pasta mixture. Cover with one third of the remaining cheeses and dot with a little butter. Repeat two more times ending with cheese. Top with freshly grated pepper. Bake 20 minutes. Serves 6.

Pasta Alberoni as served in the quaint dining rooms at Bellhill Tea House, Canning, NS. ▶

QUACO INN LOBSTER AND PASTA

THE QUACO INN, ST. MARTINS, NB

The addition of lime gives a most delightful flavour to this dish!
We served it on a bed of fresh fettucini.

1 tablespoon olive oil

2–3 garlic cloves, minced

12 ounces lobster meat in bite-size pieces
(drain well, if frozen)

1 tablespoon fresh basil, chopped (1 teaspoon
dried)

1 tablespoon fresh chives, chopped
(1 teaspoon dried)

1 tablespoon fresh oregano, (1 teaspoon
dried)

2 or 3 fresh tomatoes, cut in wedges

19-ounce can Italian-style plum tomatoes

zest and juice from 1 lime

salt and pepper, to taste

1/4 cup freshly grated Parmesan cheese

pasta of choice to serve 4

Heat olive oil in a heavy-bottomed saucepan,
add garlic and sauté until softened, being
careful not to brown. Stir in lobster and sauté
until heated through. Add herbs, fresh and
canned tomatoes, lime juice and zest. Season
with salt and pepper. Stir in Parmesan and
return to serving temperature.

Cook pasta according to package directions.
Drain and serve topped with sauce and
garnished with fresh herbs and additional
Parmesan, if desired. Serves 4.

Simply delicious, Lobster and Pasta from Quaco Inn in St. Martin's NB. ▶

LOBSTER AND DILL WITH PASTA

SCANWAY RESTAURANT, HALIFAX, NS

Unni Simensen of Scanway Restaurant prepares her dishes using only the freshest ingredients. This is a rich dish so a small quantity of the sauce goes a long way.

2 lobsters, 1 1/2 pounds each

3 cups heavy cream (35% mf)

2 tablespoons fresh dill, chopped

juice of 1 lemon

salt and pepper, to taste

4 tablespoons unsalted butter, at room temperature

10 ounces fresh fettucini

Bring a large pot of salted water to a boil. Grasp the lobsters by the back and plunge head first into the boiling water. Cover and return to a boil. Reduce heat and cook 16–18 minutes. Remove from pot and cool. Shell lobsters, cutting meat into bite-size pieces and set aside.

In a large saucepan bring cream to a boil, reduce heat to medium and boil until reduced by half. Stir in prepared lobster, dill, and lemon juice. Season with salt and pepper and simmer one minute. Remove from heat, stir in butter. Meanwhile, prepare fettucini according to package directions; drain and top with sauce. Serves 4.

Unni Simensen's Lobster and Dill with Pasta served in the warm Scandinavian atmosphere ▶ at Scanway Restauraunt.

MAIN COURSES

Behold, an array of dishes suitable for family gatherings or gala entertaining! From Dalvay-by-the-Sea's Barbecued Lobster with Red Pepper and Lime Butter to the elegant Coquille St. Jacques from the Halliburton House Inn, there is something for everyone's taste.

◄ *Seafood Stew presented by chef Brian Trainor of Nemo's Restauraunt, Halifax, NS.*

MEDITERRANEAN SEAFOOD STEW

NEMO'S RESTAURANT, HALIFAX, NS

Brian Trainor of Nemo's tells us that served with fresh crusty bread this dish makes a delicious full-bodied entrée. He suggests preparing the tomato broth ahead to enhance the flavour.

1/2 tablespoons vegetable oil

1/4 medium onion, chopped

1 large garlic clove, minced

3 ounces fresh spinach, chopped

1 teaspoon fresh coriander (optional)

salt and pepper to taste

2 tins tomatoes, crushed, 28 ounces each

1 tablespoon sugar

1/2 teaspoon fresh jalapeño pepper, seeded and finely chopped (1 teaspoon canned)

3 cups fish stock

2/3 cup water

1/2 teaspoon crushed fennel seed

1 pound fresh mussels, scrubbed and debearded

2 pounds haddock fillets, bite-size pieces

3/4 pound scallops

3/4 pound large shrimp, peeled & deveined

1/2 pound fresh clam meat

fresh parsley and lemon slices to garnish

In a large stock pot, heat oil over high heat and sauté onion and garlic until softened but not browned. Add spinach, season with coriander, salt and pepper and lower heat. Add tomatoes, sugar, jalapeño peppers and stock; simmer, stirring occasionally, for 30 minutes. Refrigerate broth for up to three days to enhance the flavour.

Reheat tomato broth over low heat. In a large saucepan bring 2/3 cup water and crushed fennel to a boil over medium heat. Add mussels, cover and steam 3 minutes. Add haddock, scallops, shrimp and clam meat, bring back to a boil and steam for an additional 2 minutes or until the mussels are open. Remove seafood from poaching liquid and add to tomato broth, discarding any mussels that have not opened.

Serve in shallow soup bowls garnished with fresh parsley and lemon slices. Serves 6–8 generously.

BARBECUED LOBSTER WITH RED PEPPER AND LIME BUTTER

DALVAY-BY-THE-SEA, DALVAY, PEI

This lobster recipe, with its subtle roasted red pepper and lime, provides a completely different flavour from boiled lobster. To complete your feast, Chef Richard Kemp, of Dalvay, includes his Jamaican Coleslaw recipe which he serves as an accompaniment.

4 lobsters, 1 to 1 1/2 pounds each

1 red bell pepper, roasted, peeled and seeded

2 tablespoons oil

1 cup butter, softened

2 limes, juice and zest

salt and pepper to taste

pinch of cayenne pepper

1/2 cup olive oil

2 cloves garlic, chopped

juice of 1 lemon

1/2 cup each fresh chives and coriander (cilantro), chopped

coarsely ground black pepper

lemon wedges as garnish

Bring a large pot of salted water to boil, plunge in lobsters for 4–6 minutes to blanch. Remove and cool lobsters until you can handle them. Cut in half, lengthwise, remove viscera, and crack claws.

Preheat oven to 425°F. Brush red pepper with oil, place on a baking sheet and roast for 15 minutes, turning several times. Remove from oven and cool. Carefully peel off pepper skin, remove seeds and chop the pepper. Place softened butter, red pepper, zest and juice of limes in a blender and process until smooth. Season with salt, pepper and cayenne. Set aside at room temperature.

Prepare marinade by combining olive oil, garlic, lemon juice, chives, coriander and black pepper. Rub thoroughly over lobster and let stand 20 minutes. Barbecue lobster flesh-side down on a hot grill until golden. Turn, brush flesh with red pepper butter and cook, shell side down for another 6-8 minutes, allowing the lobster to braise in its own juices. Arrange lobster on warm plates, top with remaining red pepper butter. Accompany lobster with a large spoonful of Jamaican Coleslaw (recipe follows) and a garnish of lemon wedges.

See Jamaican Coleslaw on following page.

JAMAICAN COLESLAW

1/4 head of red cabbage

1/4 head chinese cabbage

1 red onion

2 stalks celery

1 large carrot

1 garlic clove, minced

1/2 teaspoon ground cumin

1/2 teaspoon ground coriander seeds

1/2 teaspoon curry powder

1/2 teaspoon dijon mustard

juice of 2 limes

1/4 cup red wine vinegar

1 cup olive oil

salt and pepper, to taste

Finely slice the cabbages, onion, celery and carrot. Set aside in a large bowl. Place remaining ingredients, except salt and pepper, in a blender and process. Coat vegetables with sauce, mixing well. Season with salt and pepper. Serves 4.

Barbecued Lobster with Jamaican Coleslaw served at Dalvay-by-the-sea, Dalvay, PEI. ▶

PAN-SEARED SCALLOPS WITH BLACK OLIVE COUSCOUS, BASIL PUREE AND TOMATO OLIVE BROTH

THE INN AT BAY FORTUNE, BAY FORTUNE, PEI

Chef Michael Smith has a penchant for creating exotic entrées. Don't be intimidated! We suggest you read through the recipe, preparing each segment separately because it is not difficult and the presentation is stunning.

1 to 1 1/4 pounds large scallops

butter for searing

Tomato Olive Broth (recipe follows)

Basil Purée (recipe follows)

Black Olive Couscous (recipe follows)

Heat a heavy-bottomed skillet over high heat. Add butter and scallops and sear until the scallops are just cooked.

Prepare Tomato Olive Broth, Basil Purée and Black Olive Couscous.

Tomato Olive Broth

1 large or 2 medium vine-ripened tomatoes

1/4 cup extra virgin olive oil

salt and pepper to taste

Purée tomatoes and olive oil in a blender until very smooth, season with salt and pepper. Reserve and gently heat before serving.

Basil Purée

1 cup densely packed fresh basil leaves

1/4 cup extra virgin olive oil

Purée basil and olive oil in a blender until very smooth. Reserve and refrigerate.

Black Olive Couscous

1 7/8 cup water

1 cup black olives, chopped (preferably Kalamata)

1/4 cup extra virgin olive oil

1/2 teaspoon salt

1 cup couscous grain

Bring water, olives, oil and salt to a boil. Stir in couscous, return to a boil and immediately cover and remove from heat. Let sit for 5 minutes. Place in individual molds if desired, then serve immediately.

Assemble entrée on a platter or individual serving plates. Place Black Olive Couscous in centre of dish, then arrange scallops around the couscous. Dot each scallop with Basil Purée and serve drizzled with warmed Tomato Olive Broth. Serves 4.

Irresistible Seared Scallops with Couscous, from the Inn at Bay Fortune, PEI. ▶

FRESH STEAMED LOBSTER COMPASS ROSE

THE COMPASS ROSE INN, LUNENBURG, NS

This is how food experts Rodger and Suzanne Pike of Lunenburg's Compass Rose Inn prepare their freshly steamed lobster. They suggest that the very first thing you must do is remove the rubber bands from the lobster claws before cooking, as they transfer a rubber taste to the lobster meat.

2 lobsters, 1 pound each

Romaine leaves, for garnish

1/2 cup melted butter

1 lemon, sliced in wedges

parsley sprigs

Place a vegetable steamer in an appropriately sized pot and put in enough water to cover the bottom of the steamer. Bring the water to a hard boil, place lobsters in the steamer and cover. Cooking time will vary depending on the size of the lobsters but at the Compass Rose a 1–pound lobster is cooked in a commercial steamer for 20 minutes.

When cooked, remove the lobster from the pot and briefly cool under cold water. Crack the lobster in the kitchen for ease of eating. Place the lobster upside down. Take a cleaver and place the point at the beginning of the tail; slice down the middle breaking right through the outer shell. With the lobster still on its back, bring the cleaver sharply down on each claw and twist sideways forcing the claw shell apart.

For presentation, put two romaine leaves on a plate and place the lobster on top, with the front covering the stems of the romaine. In between the claws place a small bowl of melted butter. Position two lemon wedges where the claws join the body and parsley sprigs between the lemons and down the cut made in the tail. Take a paper towel dipped in a small amount of the melted butter and rub over the lobster shell. *Bon appetit!*

ASTICE CON FUNGHI (LOBSTER WITH WILD MUSHROOMS)

DA MAURIZIO DINING ROOM, HALIFAX, NS

The addition of wild portobello and porcini mushrooms gives this Northern Italian entrée a delicate woodsy flavour.

1 ounce dried porcini mushrooms (available in Italian markets or speciality stores)

1/2 cup white wine

4 lobsters, 1 1/2 pounds each

cooking stock (recipe follows)

1/4 cup butter

1 small onion, diced

12 ounces fresh portobello mushrooms, stems removed

2 cups tomato sauce

6 fresh basil leaves (1/4 teaspoon dried)

salt and pepper, to taste

Soak porcini in white wine and let stand for 30 minutes.

Prepare lobsters according to cooking stock directions. Carefully remove claw and tail meat from shells; keep warm.

In a large skillet melt butter, add onion and sauté until translucent. Slice portobello mushrooms 1/4-inch thick and add to onions. Sauté until tender, approximately 5 minutes. Add porcini, wine, tomato sauce, and basil, cooking until sauce is reduced and slightly thickened. Season with salt and pepper.

To serve, divide sauce between four plates, arrange lobster on top in its original shape. Serves 4.

Stock

8 cups water

4 tablespoons coarse salt

1 medium onion, quartered

1 stalk celery, chopped

1 medium carrot, chopped

2 bay leaves

1 sprig parsley

1 sprig thyme (1/4 teaspoon dried)

1 lemon, quartered

In a large stockpot combine all ingredients; bring to a boil, reduce heat and simmer 15 minutes. Return to a hard boil, plunge lobsters into water and bring back to a boil. Reduce heat and cook lobsters 20 minutes. Remove lobster and cool to room temperature.

HADDOCK FILLETS WITH LOBSTER SAUCE

BLUENOSE LODGE, LUNENBURG, NS

Grace Swan, of Bluenose Lodge, takes great care in the visual presentation of her dishes and this white haddock napped with a reddish-pink lobster sauce is a classic example of her expertise.

4–6 haddock fillets, 4–5 ounces each

1/2 onion, thinly sliced

2 teaspoons salt

1 bay leaf

3 tablespoons butter

1 tablespoon green onion

3 tablespoons flour

1 cup milk

1/3 cup reserved poaching liquid

2 ounces canned lobster paste

2 ounces chopped lobster meat

1 tablespoon chopped fresh cilantro or parsley

Place fillets in a single layer in a large skillet; add boiling water to cover. Place sliced onion, salt and bay leaf in skillet; cover and simmer until fish flakes easily when tested with a fork, about 5–8 minutes. Remove fillets to a serving platter and keep warm. Strain poaching liquid and reserve.

Heat butter in a skillet over medium heat, add green onions and gently sauté one minute. Whisk in flour, milk and 1/3 cup of the reserved poaching liquid. Bring to a boil, reduce heat and simmer until thickened. Stir in lobster paste and meat and bring back to serving temperature. Arrange fillets on plates and nap with lobster sauce. Sprinkle with cilantro or parsley to garnish. Serves 4–6.

Chef Grace Swan's Fillets with Lobster Sauce from the dining room ▶ of Bluenose Lodge, Lunenburg, NS.

CODE DI ARAGOSTA ALLA SUPREMA (LOBSTER TAILS SUPREME)

DA MAURIZIO DINING ROOM, HALIFAX, NS

If you cannot purchase individual lobster tails, it will be necessary to cook four lobsters weighing 1 1/2 pounds each, in order to have tails weighing 4–5 ounces.

1/2 cup butter, softened

3 cloves garlic, crushed

3 tablespoons parsley, chopped

4 cooked lobster tails, shelled and halved

1/2 cup white wine

salt and pepper to taste

1 cup heavy cream (35% mf)

Blend together butter, garlic and parsley until smooth.

In a skillet over medium-high heat, melt garlic butter. Add lobster tails and sauté for 3 minutes being careful not to brown butter. Remove lobster with a slotted spoon and reserve. Deglaze pan with wine, season with salt and pepper and reduce liquid by one half. Add cream and cook until the sauce is thickened. Return lobster to sauce to heat through. Serve immediately. Serve 4.

CAPPESANTE DI CHIOGGRA (SCALLOPS CHIOGGRA STYLE)

LA PERLA RESTAURANT, DARTMOUTH, NS

This is one of La Perla's acclaimed authentic Northern Italian dishes. Savour the aroma of garlic, brandy and lemon, married to the subtle taste of scallops. It's a union made in heaven!

1 1/4 pounds large scallops

2 teaspoons coarse salt

1/3 cup olive oil

2–3 medium size garlic cloves, finely chopped

12 to 15 sprigs Italian parsley, finely chopped

salt and pepper to taste

1/4 cup dry white wine

2 tablespoons brandy, slightly warmed

juice of 1 lemon

Place scallops in cold water with salt and soak for one half-hour. Heat oil in a large skillet over medium heat and sauté garlic and parsley 2 minutes. Drain scallops and pat dry. Lower heat and add scallops to skillet, cover pan and cook 3 minutes. Season with salt and pepper, add wine and let reduce by one half. Add slightly warmed brandy and flambé. Drizzle with the juice of the lemon. Serves 4.

Elegant and appetizing — Scallops Chioggra Style served in individual scallop shells ▶ at La Perla Restauraunt, Dartmouth, NS.

LOBSTER AND CHICKEN SUPREME

MARSHLANDS INN, SACKVILLE, NB

The chefs at Marshlands Inn cut the chicken and lobster pieces in medallions and serve them alternately on the plate. Drizzled with a rich sherry-flavoured cream sauce, this dish is a perfect entrée for special occasions.

2 lobsters, 1 1/2 pounds each

3 tablespoons vegetable oil

1/2 cup sherry

1 1/3 cup heavy cream (35% mf)

4 boneless chicken breasts, 4 ounces each

flour, for dusting

2 tablespoons vegetable oil (2nd amount)

salt and pepper, to taste

Bring a large kettle of salted water to a full boil. Plunge lobsters head first into water and hold under water with a wooden spoon for four minutes. Remove from water and set aside until cool enough to handle.

Separate claws and tails from lobster bodies. Remove tomalley from bodies and reserve. (Tomalley is the soft olive-green liver, found in the body of the lobster. It can be eaten alone or incorporated into sauces, and is considered a delicacy.)

Crack claws and slice tails (shells and meat) into medallions. In a large skillet, heat oil until hot and sauté lobster pieces, stirring occasionally for 2–3 minutes. Deglaze pan with sherry, bring to the boil; add cream and simmer 8–10 minutes until cooked.

Preheat oven to 400°F. Dredge chicken in flour, coating lightly. Heat oil (2nd amount) over high heat in a heavy ovenproof skillet and brown chicken, turning once. Place skillet in oven and bake 5–7 minutes until chicken is no longer pink in the centre.

With a slotted spoon remove lobster from pan. Separate meat from shells and keep warm. Return sauce to medium heat, whisk in reserved tomalley and juices and reduce until slightly thickened. Season sauce with salt and pepper. Arrange lobster and chicken on plates, topped with cream sauce. Serves 4.

Lobster and Chicken Supreme from Marshlands Inn, Sackville, NB. ▶

LOBSTER ORIENTAL

INN ON THE COVE, SAINT JOHN, NB

This entrée from Ross and Willa Mavis is a healthy choice with any vegetable combination. They often give a New Brunswick flavour to this dish by using blanched fiddleheads instead of broccoli or zucchini.

2 cups cooked lobster meat or a 12-ounce can frozen lobster

2 tablespoons canola oil

1 cup fresh mushrooms, sliced

1 cup celery, diagonally sliced

1 cup cauliflower florets

1 cup broccoli florets or sliced zucchini

1 red or yellow pepper, cubed

1/2 cup fish or chicken broth

1 tablespoon cornstarch

1 tablespoon cold water

1 tablespoon soya or oyster sauce

1/8 teaspoon hot red pepper flakes, or to taste

salt and pepper to taste

1 teaspoon dulse flakes (optional)

Coarsely chop lobster, removing cartilage or any shell pieces, set aside. In a wok or large skillet, heat canola oil over medium to high heat. Add vegetables and stir or toss quickly for 1–2 minutes. Add broth and cover to allow vegetables to steam for until crisp tender. Mix cornstarch with cold water, add soya, or oyster sauce, and hot pepper flakes. Stir into hot broth in wok and coat all vegetables. Add lobster and heat through. Sprinkle with dulse flakes and serve with rice or pasta. Serves 4.

For a low-cal gourmet dish serve Lobster Oriental, as created by Willa and Ross Mavis at the ▶ Inn on the Cove, Saint John, NB.

COQUILLE ST. JACQUES

HALLIBURTON HOUSE INN, HALIFAX, NS

Chef Maurice Pohl serves his elegant Coquille St. Jacques in individual scallop shells surrounded by piped duchess potatoes.

2 tablespoons butter

1 tablespoon lemon juice

1 to 1 1/4 pounds fresh Digby scallops

2 large garlic cloves, finely chopped

4 tablespoons dry white wine

2 tablespoons brandy or cognac

1 cup heavy cream (35% mf)

1/4 cup grated parmesan cheese

Melt butter in a skillet over medium high heat. Add lemon juice and sauté scallops and garlic until scallops are springy to the touch, about 3–5 minutes depending upon size. Remove to a warm serving plate and reserve.

Deglaze pan with wine and brandy and any juice that has formed under the scallops. Over medium heat, reduce mixture to the consistency of a thick glaze. Slowly stir in cream and simmer until sauce becomes thick. Add scallops and return to serving temperature. Serve in individual scallop shells or a shallow casserole. Sprinkle with parmesan cheese and broil until golden. Serves 4.

A classic — Coquille St. Jacques, as served at the Halliburton House Inn, Halifax ▶

LOBSTER NEWBURG

AMHERST SHORE COUNTRY INN, LORNEVILLE, NS

At the Amherst Shore Country Inn the first person of the day to make a dinner reservation may be asked to help owner Donna Laceby decide the menu for that evening.

1/3 cup butter

4 cups fresh lobster meat, in bite-size pieces

generous dash paprika

generous dash nutmeg

1/2 cup medium dry sherry

6 egg yolks, lightly beaten

2 cups heavy cream (35% mf)

Melt butter in the top of a double boiler over hot, but not boiling water. Add lobster meat and sauté gently until heated through. Add paprika, nutmeg and sherry, and return to a serving temperature. Blend egg yolks and cream with a wire whisk; add to the lobster and heat gently until hot and the sauce begins to thicken. Do not boil. Serve immediately in a puff pastry shell, over rice or with a medley of seasonal vegetables. Serves 6.

Donne Laceby's Lobster Newburg served with a medley of vegetables at Amherst Shore ▶ Country Inn, Lorneville, NS.

FILLET OF BEEF ATLANTIC

AMHERST SHORE COUNTRY INN, LORNEVILLE, NS

This has to be our all time favourite "surf and turf" recipe, given to us a number of years ago by Donna Laceby. We serve it to special friends on special occasions.

1/2 small onion, chopped

2 tablespoon butter

4 tablespoons flour

2 cups light cream (10% mf)

6 tablespoons consommé

1/4 cup dry white wine

18 medium shrimps, sliced in half lengthwise

18 scallops, sliced in half

6 beef tenderloin fillets cut 1 1/4 inch thick, 6 ounces each

In a medium skillet sauté onion in butter until slightly browned. Add flour to make a roux. Gradually whisk in blend, consommé and wine. Cook, stirring constantly, until sauce is the consistency of heavy cream. Add shellfish and keep warm.

Grill or barbecue fillets until desired degree of doneness. Pour 1/2 cup seafood sauce over each fillet. Serves 6.

SHRIMP AND SCALLOP SAUTÉ

AUBERGE LE VIEUX PRESBYTÈRE DE BOUCTOUCHE 1880, BOUCTOUCHE, NB

Marcelle Albert, chef de cuisine, serves this healthy shrimp and scallop entrée accompanied with fresh spring vegetables and a rice pilaf.

2 tablespoons butter

2 tablespoons olive oil

3–4 garlic cloves, minced

1 pound fresh mushrooms, sliced

2 tablespoons tomato paste

1/2 cup dry white wine

24 raw shrimp, peeled and deveined

1 pound scallops (halved, if large)

salt and pepper

1/3 cup fresh parsley, chopped

Melt butter with olive oil in a heavy skillet over medium heat. Add minced garlic and sauté 1 minute. Increase heat to high, add sliced mushrooms and sauté until just beginning to soften, about 5 minutes. Stir in tomato paste and wine and bring to a boil. Add shrimps and scallops and sauté until cooked through. Season with salt and pepper and sprinkle with chopped parsley. Serves 4.

Shrimp and Scallop Sauté served with a rice pilaf at Auberge le Vieux Presbytère ▼ de Bouctouche 1880, Bouctouche, NB.

INDEX

Acton's Grill and Café, Wolfville, NS 32
  Fresh Atlantic Lobster Soufflé 32
Amherst Shore Country Inn, Lorneville, NS
  Lobster Newburg 60
  Fillet of Beef Atlantic 62
Appetizers and Soups 9–17
  Atlantic Mussels in Creamy Herb Sauce 15
  Atlantic Blue Mussel Chowder 17
  Béarnaise Sauce 14
  Cozze al Forno (Broiled Mussels) 16
  Creamy Clam Chowder 16
  Dunes' Seafood Chowder with Lobster 10
  Fish Stock 10
  Gazpacho with Lobster 12
  Hot Atlantic Crab Dip 11
  Lemon Steamed Mussels 11
  Lobster Stuffed Mushroom Caps 14
Auberge Le Vieux Presbytère de Bouctouche 1880, Buctouche, NB
  Shrimp and Scallop Sauté 63
Bellhill Tea House, Canning, NS
  Pasta Alberoni 34
Blomidon Inn, Wolfville, NS
  Lobster Linguini 20
Bluenose Lodge, Lunenburg, NS
  Haddock Fillets with Lobster Sauce 50
Compass Rose, Grand Manan, NB
  Seafood Lasagna 21
Compass Rose Inn, Lunenburg, NS
  Fresh Steamed Lobster Compass Rose 48
Dalvay-by-the-Sea, Dalvay, PEI
  Barbecued Lobster with Red Pepper and Lime Butter 43
Da Maurizio Dining Room, Halifax, NS
  Astice con Funghi (Lobster with Wild Mushrooms) 49
  Code Di Aragosta Alla Suprema (Lobster Tails Supreme) 52
Drury Lane Steakhouse, Aulac, NB
  Drury Lane Club House Sandwich 22
Dufferin Inn and San Martello Diningroom, Saint John, NB
  Lobster on Potato Pancakes with Sour Cream Sauce 26

Duncreigan Country Inn, Mabou, NS
  Lobster and Scallops with Sun-dried Tomatoes in Basil Cream Sauce 31
Dunes Café and Gardens, Brackley Beach, PEI
  Dunes' Seafood Chowder with Lobster 10
Haddon Hall, Chester, NS
  Gazpacho with Lobster 12
Halliburton House Inn, Halifax, NS
  Coquille St. Jacques 58
Inn at Bay Fortune, Bay Fortune, PEI
  Pan Seared Scallops with Black Olive Couscous, Basil Purée and Tomato Olive Broth 46
Inn on the Cove, Saint John, NB
  Lobster Oriental 56
Inn on the Lake, Waverley, NS 28
  Lobster Toast Points 28
La Perla Restaurant, Dartmouth, NS
  Cappesante di Chioggra (Scallops Chioggra Style) 52
  Cozze al Forno (Broiled Mussels) 16
Main Course 41–63
  Astice con Funghi (Lobster with Wild Mushrooms) 49
  Barbecued Lobster with Red Pepper and Lime Butter 43
  Basil Purée 46
  Black Olive Couscous 46
  Cappesante di Chioggra (Scallops Chioggra Style) 52
  Code Di Aragosta Alla Suprema (Lobster Tails Supreme) 52
  Coquille St. Jacques 58
  Fillet of Beef Atlantic 62
  Fresh Steamed Lobster Compass Rose 48
  Haddock Fillets with Lobster Sauce 50
  Jamaican Coleslaw 44
  Lobster and Chicken Supreme 54
  Lobster Oriental 56
  Lobster Sauce 50
  Lobster Newburg 60
  Mediterranean Seafood Stew 42
  Pan Seared Scallops with Black Olive Couscous, Basil Purée and Tomato Olive Broth 46
  Shrimp and Scallop Sauté 63

  Tomato Olive Broth 46
Marshlands Inn, Sackville, NB
  Lobster and Chicken Supreme 54
Mountain Gap Inn and Resort, Smith's Cove, NS
  Lobster Roll 24
Murray Manor Bed and Breakfast, Yarmouth, NS
  Nova Scotia-Style Creamed Lobster 28
Nemo's Restaurant, Halifax, NS
  Mediterranean Seafood Stew 42
Pasta and Lighter Fare 19–39
  Basic Crêpe Recipe 30
  Crab Crêpes with Lemon Caper Sauce 30
  Drury Lane Club House Sandwich 22
  Fresh Atlantic Lobster Soufflé 32
  Lemon Caper Sauce 30
  Lobster and Scallops with Sun-dried Tomatoes in Basil Cream Sauce 31
  Lobster Roll 24
  Lobster Toast Points 28
  Lobster and Dill with Pasta 38
  Lobster Linguini 20
  Lobster on Potato Pancakes with Sour Cream Sauce 26
  Nova Scotia-Style Creamed Lobster 28
  Pasta Alberoni 34
  Quaco Inn Lobster and Pasta 36
  Seafood Lasagna 21
  Sour Cream Sauce 26
Off-Broadway Café, The, Charlottetown, PEI
  Lobster Stuffed Mushroom Caps 14
  Béarnaise Sauce 14
Quaco Inn, St. Martins, NB
  Quaco Inn Lobster and Pasta 36
Scanway Restaurant, Halifax, NS
  Lobster and Dill with Pasta 38
Shaw's Hotel, Brackley Beach, PEI
  Creamy Clam Chowder 16